COMBINATIONS

# What teens and others are saying about

# COMBINATIONS
## Opening the Door to
## Student Leadership

\*   \*   \*   \*   \*

"This book helped me take action as a student leader – it's motivating and full of truth."

*– Abbie, age 15*

"At long last a definitive book on leadership! A practical and user friendly text for leadership classes, *Combinations: Opening the Door to Student Leadership*, is sure to become the gold standard resource for motivating and developing leaders. Filled with stories, questions and action steps, this book is a "must have" for anyone involved in leadership training. This book delivers!"

*– Marsha Hirsch*
*Middle School Principal*
*Pembroke Hill School, Kansas City, MO*

"Inspiring, moving and very powerful. It taught me how important it is to live life to the fullest."

*– Allison, age 16*

"Ed Gerety has presented six fundamental principles for leadership development and life itself. The concepts in *Combinations: Opening the Door to Student Leadership* provide the blueprint for improved leadership skills and a more successful life. I highly recommend it!"

*– Donald C. Larsen*
*Executive Director Emeritus*
*Wisconsin Association of School Councils, Inc.*

"Full of ideas, inspiring stories and real life examples...thank you for helping me grow as a leader."
*– Jeffrey, age 16*

"Ed Gerety has been motivating and inspiring students and adults with his presentations at school assemblies, state conventions, and national conferences for more than a decade. *Combinations: Opening the Door to Student Leadership* is a guide for successful living that can be used by every high school and middle level student."
*– Les Anderson*
*Executive Director*
*North Dakota Association of Student Councils*

"This is an incredibly fun and enjoyable book. I would recommend it to anyone who is looking for an inspiring read."
*– Emily, age 18*

"I have known Ed Gerety since he first started as a professional speaker and leadership trainer. He came up through the ranks as a student leader and he 'walks the talk.' *Combinations: Opening the Door to Student Leadership* provides readers, who have not heard Ed speak, with an opportunity to experience his wisdom and learn from his experiences. It is a fast read for busy student leaders and their advisers. In addition, the action steps at the end of each chapter provide an opportunity for students to put to use what they have read. I highly recommend Ed's book for student leaders and for advisers to use with leadership classes."
*– Rocco Marano*
*Director*
*National Association of Student Councils*
*National Honor Society/National Jr. Honor Society*

"Full of real life examples of how teens can make a difference in the world today. Two thumbs up!"

*– Julie, age 15*

"Ed Gerety is one of the most outstanding keynote speakers we have had at the KIDS PLUS Conference. He has an incredible talent for connecting with young people and convincing them that mutual respect and care for one another is the foundation of positive leadership. Ed is genuine and sincere. His infectious energy literally captivates the audience and motivates youth and adults to put his powerful message into action."

*– Lynn Haglin*
*Vice President/KIDS PLUS Director*
*Northland Foundation*

"Inspiring and motivating to the human heart and spirit. You will grow and become a stronger leader after reading this book. I know I did!"

*– Kate, age 18*

"Ed Gerety's openness, exuberance and enthusiasm for life come through in this book for student leaders. Ed has a unique gift to speak to teenagers in simple, clear and compelling language. Young people know instantly that Ed is on their side and that they can trust his advice and message. Through personal stories and practical tips, Ed shows young people valuable combinations to unlock a positive future."

*– Penny Wells*
*Executive Director*
*SADD (Students Against Destructive Decisions/*
*Students Against Driving Drunk)*

# COMBINATIONS

## OPENING THE DOOR
## TO
## STUDENT LEADERSHIP

# ED GERETY

WHALEBACK
PUBLISHING

# Combinations

## Opening the Door to
## Student Leadership

ISBN 0-9725938-3-7

Bulk rate discounted purchasing is available through
contacting the publisher, contact information below.

Cover design and layout by Jim Weems, Ad Graphics, Inc.
Photography by Austin Studios
Logo design by Mark Healey, GullReef Communications, LLC

Printed in the United States of America.

PUBLISHED BY WHALEBACK PUBLISHING
*a subsidiary of Gerety Presentations*
4 Captain's Way
Exeter, NH 03833
800-207-2580
www.whalebackpublishing.com
www.geretypresentations.com

WHALEBACK
PUBLISHING

*To Mom and Dad*

For always believing in
me and my dreams

# Contents

Acknowledgments. . . . . . . . . . . . . . . . . . . . . . . . . . . . . . . . . . . . 13
About the Author. . . . . . . . . . . . . . . . . . . . . . . . . . . . . . . . . . . . 15
Introduction . . . . . . . . . . . . . . . . . . . . . . . . . . . . . . . . . . . . . . 17

COMBINATION 1: **GRATITUDE** . . . . . . . . . . . . . . . . . . . . . . . 19
    You make the call. . . . . . . . . . . . . . . . . . . . . . . . . . . . . . . . 21
    Speak from your heart . . . . . . . . . . . . . . . . . . . . . . . . . . . . . 25
    Look to this Day. . . . . . . . . . . . . . . . . . . . . . . . . . . . . . . . . 26
    Seize the day . . . . . . . . . . . . . . . . . . . . . . . . . . . . . . . . . . . 27
    Present Tense . . . . . . . . . . . . . . . . . . . . . . . . . . . . . . . . . . . 30
    Opening the Door to Student Leadership: Gratitude . . . . . 32
    Action Steps. . . . . . . . . . . . . . . . . . . . . . . . . . . . . . . . . . . . 33
    Leadership Challenge. . . . . . . . . . . . . . . . . . . . . . . . . . . . . . 39

COMBINATION 2: **ATTITUDE** . . . . . . . . . . . . . . . . . . . . . . . . 41
    Attitude is a choice. . . . . . . . . . . . . . . . . . . . . . . . . . . . . . . 43
    Dreams into action . . . . . . . . . . . . . . . . . . . . . . . . . . . . . . . 45
    Don't Quit . . . . . . . . . . . . . . . . . . . . . . . . . . . . . . . . . . . . . 46
    In your own words . . . . . . . . . . . . . . . . . . . . . . . . . . . . . . . 47
    Leap to success. . . . . . . . . . . . . . . . . . . . . . . . . . . . . . . . . . 47
    You can always go further than you think you can!. . . . . . 49
    A four-star attitude . . . . . . . . . . . . . . . . . . . . . . . . . . . . . . 51
    Opening the Door to Student Leadership: Attitude . . . . . . 52
    Action Steps. . . . . . . . . . . . . . . . . . . . . . . . . . . . . . . . . . . . 53
    Leadership Challenge. . . . . . . . . . . . . . . . . . . . . . . . . . . . . . 59

COMBINATION 3: **GOALS** . . . . . . . . . . . . . . . . . . . . . . . . . . . 61
    Reach for the stars . . . . . . . . . . . . . . . . . . . . . . . . . . . . . . . 63
    The courage to soar: setting and achieving your goals . . . 66
    Success is a journey not a destination . . . . . . . . . . . . . . . 69
    Risk . . . . . . . . . . . . . . . . . . . . . . . . . . . . . . . . . . . . . . . . . 72
    Opening the Door to Student Leadership: Goals . . . . . . . . 74
    Action Steps. . . . . . . . . . . . . . . . . . . . . . . . . . . . . . . . . . . . 75
    Leadership Challenge. . . . . . . . . . . . . . . . . . . . . . . . . . . . . . 81

COMBINATION 4: **RESPECT** . . . . . . . . . . . . . . . . . . . . . . . . 83
    A small point makes a big mark. . . . . . . . . . . . . . . . . . . . 85
    The power to choose . . . . . . . . . . . . . . . . . . . . . . . . . . . 91
    Respect for yourself and one another. . . . . . . . . . . . . . . 93
    Character . . . . . . . . . . . . . . . . . . . . . . . . . . . . . . . . . . . 94
    Actions speak louder than words . . . . . . . . . . . . . . . . . . 95
    Opening the Door to Student Leadership: Respect . . . . . . 98
    Action Steps. . . . . . . . . . . . . . . . . . . . . . . . . . . . . . . . . 99
    Leadership Challenge. . . . . . . . . . . . . . . . . . . . . . . . . . 105

COMBINATION 5: **KINDNESS** . . . . . . . . . . . . . . . . . . . . . . 107
    The Golden Rule . . . . . . . . . . . . . . . . . . . . . . . . . . . . . 109
    A pledge for kindness. . . . . . . . . . . . . . . . . . . . . . . . . . 109
    Making a difference . . . . . . . . . . . . . . . . . . . . . . . . . . . 112
    Little Champions . . . . . . . . . . . . . . . . . . . . . . . . . . . . . 115
    Watch your thoughts. . . . . . . . . . . . . . . . . . . . . . . . . . . 116
    Opening the Door to Student Leadership: Kindness . . . . 117
    Action Steps. . . . . . . . . . . . . . . . . . . . . . . . . . . . . . . . 119
    Leadership Challenge. . . . . . . . . . . . . . . . . . . . . . . . . . 125

COMBINATION 6: **BELIEVE** . . . . . . . . . . . . . . . . . . . . . . . . 127
    A dream come true . . . . . . . . . . . . . . . . . . . . . . . . . . . 129
    Teenagers Are Amazing . . . . . . . . . . . . . . . . . . . . . . . . 132
    Personal best. . . . . . . . . . . . . . . . . . . . . . . . . . . . . . . . 133
    Rising to the challenge. . . . . . . . . . . . . . . . . . . . . . . . . 135
    Seeds of wisdom . . . . . . . . . . . . . . . . . . . . . . . . . . . . . 140
    Opening the Door to Student Leadership: Believe . . . . . 144
    Action Steps. . . . . . . . . . . . . . . . . . . . . . . . . . . . . . . . 145
    Leadership Challenge. . . . . . . . . . . . . . . . . . . . . . . . . . 151

SUMMARY: **Combinations:**
**Opening the Door to Student Leadership** . . . . . . . . . . . . . . 153

Recommended Reading List . . . . . . . . . . . . . . . . . . . . . . . . . 157
Contact Information . . . . . . . . . . . . . . . . . . . . . . . . . . . . . . . 160

# Acknowledgments

To Joanne, Mark, and Steve for your lifelong loyalty and friendship.

To Rick Gregg, Dick O'Donnell, and Coleen Kelley your insights, honesty, and suggestions contributed significantly to this book. Thank you for your encouragement, time, and support. I am grateful to call you my friends.

To Don Larsen, Elena Zongrone, Les Anderson, Judi Riley, Terry Ragus, Clem Dugan, Sue Haas, Al Cormier, Andy Costanzo and Marsha Hirsch. Your friendship, guidance and generosity are a gift.

To the professional speakers and authors who have had a positive influence in my life. You continue to inspire me. In particular, Kevin Wanzer, Eric Chester, Craig Hillier, Snowden McFall, Mark Scharenbroich, and Dr. Earl Reum.

To the students, teachers, coaches and parents that I have had the opportunity to work with, thank you for making a difference in my life and for sharing your stories of triumph and courage.

To my family and friends who are the foundation of love and support in my life.

To my wife Suzanne – you are my soul mate and best friend. Thank you for making every day an adventure and a life filled with possibilities.

# About the Author

Ed Gerety is one of the top professional youth speakers and leadership trainers in the United States. His passion, humor, and ability to connect with the hearts and minds of his audience has inspired people in all 50 states, Canada, and Europe reaching over one million people and counting. His books and presentations focus on respect, character, appreciation, leadership, attitude, and making a difference.

Ed is a contributing author of three books for teens, *Teen Power Too*, *Teen Power and Beyond*, and *Go M.A.D! (Make A Difference): Real Stuff Real Teens Can Do To Make A Real Impact in an Unreal World*. He has also published an inspirational folk tale entitled *The Special Frog*.

He received his Bachelor of Arts degree in Communications from the University of New Hampshire and has completed the Boston Marathon three times. Ed lives in Exeter, New Hampshire and is married to his best friend, Suzanne.

# Introduction

What is your locker combination? Do you forget it sometimes? Does it not open sometimes because you are off by just one number? Are you the only one who knows it or do you trust another with the combination?

We all have different combinations. The locks may look the same, but what opens them is different, unique, and special to that one particular lock. As a student leader, you have to know the combinations to many things, not just to your locker. Academics, friends, family, school activities, and relationships all have combinations that you are trying to learn and understand. This is both exciting and challenging.

In this book, you will discover and learn the combinations that will help you meet this challenge and open the door to student leadership. They are principles that will empower you to lead with character, make positive choices, and take action toward your goals and dreams.

It is important to read the book from start to finish because the combinations build on each other. Each chapter includes action steps and a leadership challenge, which are designed for you to practice and become a master of that particular combination. I encourage you to go all out on the exercises. This book is like your life – you will get out of it what you put into it. Have fun!

COMBINATION

# Gratitude

**"As we express our gratitude,
we must never forget
that the highest appreciation
is not to utter words,
but to live by them."**

*– John Fitzgerald Kennedy*

*Combinations*

# You make the call

$I$f you had one hour to live, who would you call? What would you say? And why haven't you done it? I recently asked this question to one thousand high school students at a student leadership conference. A young man in the front row nervously raised his hand and answered, "I'd call my mom."

At that point I invited the young man to join me up on stage. He stood next to me and looked out cautiously at the excited audience as I challenged him and said, "Let's call your mom right now."

He accepted the challenge and dialed his mom's number, on the cell phone I provided, as all of his peers listened carefully for what would happen next. She answered. It was clear that the young man was nervous, his hand began to shake a little, and he courageously told his mom those three important words, "I love you."

As a teenager today, it can be easy to take so many simple,

**"If you had one hour to live,
who would you call?
What would you say?
And why haven't you done it?"**

*– Ed Gerety*

yet special things for granted. Your life is fast paced, hectic, and sometimes stressful with the demands of school, grades, homework, sports, activities, relationships, jobs and more. In the midst of your busy schedule it can be easy to forget that there are millions of people your age who do not have the same opportunities or abilities that you may have. They may not live in a free country or have the ability to see, hear, or walk.

I will never forget the day when Brett, a blind sixth grader, came up to me at the end of one of my presentations. He asked me if he could get an idea of what I looked like. Curiously, I said yes and the next thing I knew, Brett took both of his little hands, reached up, and put them lightly on my face.

After a few moments I asked, "Ok Brett what do I look like?" He gave me a big smile as he took both of his hands and put them on the top of my head. He replied, "Well, you are about this tall." We both began to laugh. It was at that moment that I could see that Brett had a tremendous amount of gratitude for the abilities that he still had. He may never see the ocean, the falling snow, or the face of his parents. However, his appreciation for the abilities he has helps him to be an effective leader. Brett knows living each day with gratitude will help him overcome his challenges and make his dreams a reality.

**"Lead with an awareness and appreciation for your abilities and for the people in your life."**

*– Ed Gerety*

# Speak from your heart

Unfortunately, for many of us, the only time that we realize how often we forget to be grateful for all that we have in our lives is when we lose someone close to us or when a tragedy happens. Shortly after I graduated from high school I lost my grandmother, grandfather, and a good friend. When we lose someone close to us we often have regrets about what we wish we could have said or done. Saying to ourselves, "I wish that I called that person more often, wrote them more letters, or been more kind and patient." We wish that we told that person those three words that are sometimes the hardest words to say but are the most important words of all, "I love you."

I know that as we get older it seems kind of funny to say that, but do you remember when we were little kids? Everywhere we went we would share with people exactly how we felt. We had no problem saying, "I love you!" We were open and honest with our feelings.

As we get older – I'm not sure at what age or at what grade it happens – those words of "I love you," or "I care about you," and "you are special to me" are said less and less. Until one day we just say to ourselves, "Oh, that person knows that I love them and appreciate them," or "I see them every day so I don't need to say how I feel, they already know." We often don't realize how important it is to express our feelings until it's too late.

### *Look to this Day*

Look to this day;
For it is life,
The very life of life.
In its brief course lies all
The realities and verities of existence,
The bliss of growth,
The splendor of action,
The glory of power –
For yesterday is but a dream
And tomorrow is only a vision.
But today, well lived,
Makes every yesterday a dream of happiness
And every tomorrow a vision of hope.
Look well, therefore, to this day.

*– Sanskrit Proverb*

Jennifer was a senior in high school when she experienced this first hand. Her best friend was killed in a car accident. One month after her best friend was killed, her mother died of cancer. Jennifer shared with me how much she missed her mom and her friend and how she thought of them everyday. I asked her what she would tell other students her age about what she had learned from this challenging time in her life. She answered, "I realize now how precious life is and at any moment it can be gone. It is so important to make the most out of each day and to let people know how much you care about them and love them."

## Seize the day

It is not only our busy lives that can cause us to sometimes forget to be thankful for our abilities and for the people in our life. It can also be because many of us get so upset about what happened in the past or so worried about what is going to happen in the future that we miss out on what is happening today; right now.

John, a tenth grader, shared with me that when his girlfriend broke up with him during the school year he was upset and angry about it for several months. As a result, his success in the classroom and on the soccer field began to decline. His friends were getting

**"Yesterday's the past, tomorrow's the future, but today is a gift. That's why it's called the present."**

*– Bill Keane*

tired of him being depressed and always talking about his ex-girlfriend. John said, "I could see that I was living in the past and as a result I was missing out on once in a lifetime opportunities with my friends. My chances of getting a soccer scholarship were being hurt because I was not concentrating on the field or in the classroom. I realized that the past is history and the only way that I'm going to succeed is to learn from the past, then let go of it and begin to put all my effort into today right now."

If it is not the past that some of us are always worried about then sometimes it's the future. We find ourselves saying things such as:

"When I get my license, then I will be happy."

"When I do well on the SATs next year, then I will enjoy school."

"When I graduate and go to college then I will make friends."

"When I'm eighteen then I will be able to have my freedom."

"All I want to do is get married and have children."

"I can't wait until I can move away and get a job then I will appreciate life!"

# *Present Tense*

It was spring
But it was summer I wanted,
The warm days and the great outdoors
It was summer
But it was fall I wanted
The colorful leaves and the cool, dry air
It was fall
But it was winter that I wanted
The beautiful snow
And the joy of the holiday season
It was winter
But it was spring I wanted
The warmth and the blossoming of nature
I was a child
But it was adulthood I wanted
The freedom, and the respect,
I was 20
But it was 30 I wanted
To be mature
And sophisticated
I was middle aged
But it was 20 I wanted
The youth and the free spirit
I was retired but it was middle age I wanted
The presence of mind
Without limitations
My life was over
But I never got what I wanted

*– Jason Lehman*

If we continue to keep wishing for and living in the future then we will miss out on once in a lifetime opportunities.

Kristin, in her first year in college, realized that she had done just that. "All through high school I only talked and thought about how I couldn't wait to go college. I pretended that I was more mature than everyone else and that high school was dumb. I only worried about getting good grades. I didn't get involved in any school activities or really make an effort to have any friends. I remember sitting at my high school graduation feeling very sad. It was at that moment I realized I was so concerned about the future that I missed out on many great experiences and friendships."

Unfortunately, Kristin cannot go back and make up for time that has gone by. She now realizes that it is important to be excited about the future – it will be here soon enough. In the meantime she is going to make every second count and enjoy the moment!

## Combination 1:

# Gratitude

### *Opening the Door to Student Leadership*

The expressions of gratitude such as:
saying "I love you," being apprecia-
tive of your freedoms and abilities,
living in the present moment, and
being thankful for all that you have
is essential to being a great leader.
People will not care how much you
know until they know how much you
care. That caring starts with you leading with gratitude.

# Action Steps

## Combination 1:
## Gratitude

OPENING THE DOOR TO
STUDENT LEADERSHIP

## Combination 1:
# Gratitude

The following action steps are designed for you to practice the combination GRATITUDE and open the door to student leadership.

**GRATITUDE**: (grat' i-tood) *n*. thankful appreciation.

---

**"Two roads diverged in a wood, and I–
I took the one less traveled by,
and that has made all the difference."**

*– Robert Frost*

---

- Write a letter to a loved one or friend letting them know how much you care about them and appreciate them. Mail the letter after you've written it.

- List five people that you are going to call to tell them how important they are in your life. What was their reaction when you called them? How did it make you feel?

- List ten things you are grateful for in your life right now.

- Describe one of the most beautiful things that you have ever seen.

  _____

  _____

  _____

  _____

  _____


- What experience/adventure have you had for which you are grateful?

  _____

  _____

  _____

  _____

  _____


- Give three examples of ways you can seize the day and be more present in the moment.

  _____

  _____

  _____

  _____

  _____

- Create your own quote or inspirational thought
  about Combination 1: GRATITUDE.

  _____

  _____

  _____

  _____

# Leadership Challenge:

Begin keeping a daily journal where
you write your thoughts, feelings,
goals, dreams and experiences.

COMBINATION

# Attitude

"Most people are like falling
leaves that drift and turn in the air,
flutter, and fall to the ground.
But a few others are like the stars
which travel one defined path:
no wind reaches them,
they have within themselves
their guide and path."

*– Hermann Hesse*

*Combinations*

# Attitude is a choice

To be an outstanding leader you must have an outstanding attitude. This does not mean that you just look at everything around you as being positive and perfect. It does mean that you make a choice about how you are going to take on each day. It's how you approach the experiences that are presented to you. The important thing to remember is that unless we take action toward our goals and dreams with our outstanding attitude, it is just a hopeful idea, a wishful thought.

**"Unless we take action toward our goals and dreams with our outstanding attitude, it is just a hopeful idea, a wishful thought."**

*– Ed Gerety*

## Dreams into action

Mike was a ninth grader who was struggling in school and having a hard time getting along with his teachers. He started to realize that the more he got down on himself and the more negative he became his grades only got worse. Not wanting to stay back or completely fail, Mike began to turn his attitude around by refocusing on his goals and dreams. He made a list of all the things that he wanted to achieve in life. In doing this, Mike was reminded of how he had always wanted to go to college. He knew that if he was going to achieve this goal, he had to not only change his attitude but his grades too.

Mike started to go in for extra help after school and realized that his teachers were there to help him. He began to look at school as a game in which he had the choice in how he wanted to play it. Instead of complaining he looked for ways that he could take action and where he could get help and support. His positive attitude resulted in him not only improving his grades but also getting one step closer toward achieving his goal.

## *Don't Quit*

When things go wrong, as they sometimes will,
When the road you're trudging seems all up hill,
When the funds are low, and the debts are high,
and you want to smile, but you have to sigh,
when care is pressing you down a bit,
rest if you must, but don't you quit,

Life is odd with its twists and turns,
As everyone of us sometimes learns,
and many a failure turns about,
when we might have won had we stuck it out,
Don't give up though the pace seems slow,
you may succeed with another blow.

Success is failure turned inside out,
the silver tint of the clouds of doubt,
and you never can tell how close you are,
it may be near when it seems so far;
So stick to the fight when you're hardest hit,
It's when things seem worse, that you must not quit.

*– Author Unknown*

## In your own words

There are all kinds of ways to describe what a positive attitude looks like. Here are just a few:

"Having a positive attitude is not letting others make you feel down."– Katie, seventh grader

"A positive attitude means not giving up and looking at ways that I can get help instead of complaining." – Brian, eleventh grader

"A positive attitude is when you look at the bright side of things and know that if you are having a difficult time, things will get better if you keep on trying, learn from your mistakes and believe in yourself." – Emily, twelfth grader

What does a positive attitude look like for you?

## Leap to success

In high school, I heard a great folktale about having a positive attitude.

One day, three frogs were hopping along at a farm when they came across a big bucket of milk and decided to jump in. They started swimming around, laughing having a great time. The frogs got thirsty and started drinking the milk. As they continued drinking, they found themselves at the bottom of the bucket.

Along came four other frogs that became curious when they heard all kinds of noise coming from the bucket. They hopped up around the edge of the bucket to see what was going on. One of the frogs looked down and yelled, "Hey, you three frogs down there, look how far down you are. You drank all that milk and now you are way down at the bottom. You're not going to be able to get out. You're going to drown!"

The first two frogs in the bucket looked up, heard this, and start panicking and trying to jump out of the bucket. The four mean frogs started yelling, "You are not going to make it! You're going to drown. Give up!"

The third frog in the bucket suddenly saw the two other frogs jumping wildly to get out. She could see the four frogs all around the edge, waving their arms and kicking their legs. The third frog then started trying to get out of the bucket.

The four mean frogs were still yelling, "You're not going to make it! You're going to drown. Give up!" Sadly, the first two frogs gave up and drowned, believing what those four frogs told them.

The third frog was still trying to get out of the bucket, and was completely out of breath. She looked up saw the four mean frogs still waving their arms yelling and screaming.

She closed her eyes and said, "I know I can do it!" With one last giant leap, the third frog jumped out of the bucket.

The reason why the third frog got out was because she was deaf. The whole time the four frogs were yelling and screaming and waving their arms, the third deaf frog, with her positive attitude, just looked up and said to herself, "Hey, look at those four frogs up there. They must really want me to get out of the bucket. She thought they were yelling, "Come on get out of the bucket! You can make it don't give up! You can do it!"

Be deaf to those people who say you cannot achieve the positive things that you want. Keep your ears open to those who believe in you. Having a positive attitude is one of the most powerful combinations you have to help you believe in yourself and make a difference as a leader.

## You can always go further than you think you can!

It is important to have goals and dreams. The only way that we can reach them is if we put 110% into today, right now.

Two days before Christmas, fifteen-year-old Scott was involved in a horrible car crash that resulted in one of his legs having to be amputated. This was devastating news to Scott and his family because Scott's dream of playing professional basketball seemed to be shattered. Scott, however, refused to give up his dream. Despite words of caution from his doctors, he slowly began to work towards his goal of playing basketball again. Every day he went through grueling exercises at physical therapy so that he could adjust to his prosthetic leg. He dedicated himself to practice, shooting hoops in his driveway each day. Many believed he was only setting himself up for disappointment, but Scott knew in his heart that one day he would make it back to the court and the game he loved.

Through an amazing amount of hard work and determination, only one year after the accident, Scott made his high school varsity basketball team. A huge crowd gathered in the gymnasium to witness Scott's miraculous return to the court. In the first game of the season, Scott scored eight points and played solid defense!

Although he did not reach his ultimate goal of playing professional basketball, Scott achieved something even greater. Through this experience, Scott discovered that success in life is not always about finishing first, having the highest grades, or even becoming a professional athlete. Real success is defined by the person you become and what you experience along the way.

## A four-star attitude

Rick Allen, the drummer for the rock band Def Leppard, knows the power of a positive attitude. After having lost his arm in an automobile accident he did not give up his passion for playing the drums. Instead, he had a custom designed set of drums made for him and was back playing with the band several months after the accident.

As a student leader, there are four things you can do every day to take your attitude to the next level.

- **Surround yourself with positive people:** those who support you, encourage you, and bring out the best in you.

- **Surround yourself with positive things**: read inspirational books, watch movies and listen to music with a positive or uplifting message.

- **Be aware of your physiology:** research shows that your posture, how you sit, and how you move influences your attitude either in a positive or negative way.

- **Find humor in the situation**: sometimes things can be taken too seriously. Laughter can often be the best way to deal with a challenging situation.

# Combination 2:

# Attitude

### *Opening the Door to*
### *Student Leadership*

It's your choice to have an outstanding attitude and to take action toward your goals and dreams. It takes courage to be yourself and to not measure your self worth by your position, your title, or by what others may or may not think of you. Success is not measured by how well known you are, but how well respected you are. Never give up!

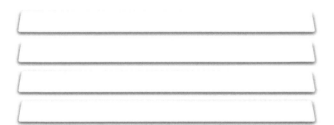

# Action Steps

## Combination 2:
## Attitude

**OPENING THE DOOR TO
STUDENT LEADERSHIP**

## Combination 2:
# Attitude

The following action steps are designed for you to practice the combination ATTITUDE and open the door to student leadership.

**ATTITUDE:** (at' e tood) *n.* a manner, showing one's feelings or thoughts.

---

**"A positive attitude is like a paint brush
that allows you to color the world the
way you want it to be."**

*– Steve Gerety*

---

- Who are five people that you know who have an outstanding attitude? What can you learn from them?

  _____

  _____

  _____

  _____

- What inspires you?

  _____

  _____

  _____

  _____

- What are three things that you can do right now to begin to have an outstanding attitude?

  _____

  _____

  _____

  _____

*Combinations*

- What is something you have accomplished through having a positive attitude?

- Who is a role model that you admire? What qualities do they have?

- Create your own quote or inspirational thought about Combination 2: ATTITUDE.

## Leadership Challenge:

Put positive pictures, quotes, and words that inspire you in your bedroom, inside your locker at school, on the cover of your books, and on your refrigerator.

COMBINATION

3

# Goals

**"Obstacles are those frightful things you see when you take your eyes off your goal."**

*– Henry Ford*

*Combinations*

# Reach for the stars

When I was a college student, I set a goal to run the 26.2-mile Boston Marathon. After six months of training, the day had finally arrived. I was nervous and excited.

There were times during the race when my legs began to cramp up and I thought that I may not finish. Instead of stopping, I told myself to stay focused on my goal and concentrate on taking one step forward at a time. It was this focus and concentration that helped me finally cross the finish line.

After a race, we often hear about the person who finished first and those who finished in the top ten. Many of us though, did not hear about another runner who also ran the Boston Marathon. Meredith did not cross the finish line the year that she ran the Boston marathon

**"Turning your dreams into a reality,
takes attitude, focus,
determination, and discipline."**

*– Ed Gerety*

until 8:30 pm. The race started at 12:00 in the afternoon. Does it mean that Meredith did not reach her goal because she didn't finish with an award winning time? No way!

Meredith put forth her best effort, and if you put forth your best effort toward whatever goal you are trying to achieve, then you did succeed. Why? You are a better person inside because you made that attempt. Do not let anyone tell you differently. No matter what goal it is that you are trying to achieve, there are going to be challenges, setbacks, and disappointments. It is at these times that staying focused on your goal and having a positive attitude is more important than ever. Achieving our goals and turning our dreams into a reality is not easy, it takes an outstanding attitude, focus, determination, and discipline.

# The courage to soar: setting and achieving your goals

Research has shown that those who write down their goals are more likely to achieve them compared to people who don't write them down. This goal setting formula is designed for you to follow as you take action toward your goals.

**What goal do I want to achieve?**

**Examples:**  (a) I want to make the softball team.

(b) I want to earn better grades.

(c) I want to play the electric guitar.

**How can I make my goal as specific as possible?**

**Examples:**  (a) I will make the varsity softball team in my sophomore year as a pitcher.

(b) I will earn a B average or better in my five subjects this school year.

(c) I will learn how to play my favorite song on the electric guitar in one month.

## What resources and skills do I currently have that will help me in reaching my goal?

**Examples**:  (a) I have a strong arm; I have an older sister who is pitcher in college that can help me.

(b) I can go in after school for extra help; I can find a friend who does well in that subject and study with him.

(c) I know a lot about music; my friend already plays the guitar; I have a neighbor who gives guitar lessons.

## What mini goals do I need to set in order to achieve my goal?

**Examples:**  (a) Be able to curl 30 pounds on each arm. Get pointers from my sister on what skills I can improve on. Meet with the coach.

(b) Study for my test on Friday with my friend in class. Schedule time to meet with my teachers. Use my school planner to organize my assignments.

(c) Sign up for lessons. Buy an electric guitar. Learn the song from my friend who plays the guitar.

**By what date do I want to accomplish each mini goal?**

**Examples:**     (a) Be able to curl 30 pounds on each arm by March 1st. Get pointers from my sister on what I can improve on by March 7th. Meet with the coach by March 14th.

(b) Study for my test on Friday with my friend in class by Wednesday evening. Schedule time to meet with my teachers by Thursday after school. Use my school planner to organize my assignments by Friday.

(c) Sign up for lessons by June 2nd. Buy an electric guitar by June 7th. Learn the song from my friend who plays the guitar by June 30th.

**By what date do I want to have my major goal achieved?**

**Examples:**     (a) I will make the varsity softball team in my sophomore year as a pitcher by the start of the season on April 1st.

(b) I will earn a B average or better in my five subjects this school year when grades are sent on June 15th.

(c) I will begin taking lessons this month and learn how to play the song on my electric guitar by June 30th.

**Take action with an outstanding attitude and evaluate your progress.**

# Success is a journey not a destination

I shared the following statement with a group of student leaders.

If you put forth your best effort toward your goal, then you did achieve it. You are a better person because you made that attempt. You have made your school or team better because you made that attempt. Don't ever let anyone tell you differently.

At that point, Laura, one of the students, said, "That's ridiculous; put forth your best effort and whether or not you reach your goal it's ok because you're a better person because you made that attempt. I don't agree with that at all."

I asked Laura to give me an example. She said, "I'm a senior, and in the beginning of the year my goal was to be captain of the soccer team. I didn't get it and you're telling me that's ok because I'm a better person because I made that attempt."

**Ed:** Did you write your goal down and were you clear and specific?

**Laura:** Yes, I was clear and specific.

**Ed:** What were the mini-goals that you set for yourself?

**"Only those who dare to fail greatly
can ever achieve greatly."**

*– Robert Francis Kennedy*

*Combinations*

**Laura**:

- I brought all of my grades up from a C average to a B average because at this school you cannot be captain of any team unless you have a B average or better.

- I met with every player before the season started to find out what their individual and team goals were.

- I worked out every day and ate healthy.

- In my mind, I visualized being captain of the team.

- I had a positive attitude.

**Laura:** I did all of that and still I didn't achieve my goal.

**Ed:** I know the season is over, but how did your team do?

**Laura:** We did ok.

*Her friend sitting next to her then spoke up and said, "We didn't just do ok, our team made it to the state finals for the first time in school history, we lost but it was still a great season."*

**Ed:** How did you do on an individual basis?

# *RISK*

To laugh is to risk appearing the fool.
To weep is to risk appearing sentimental.
To reach out for another is to risk involvement.
To expose your feelings is to risk
exposing your true self.

To place your ideas, your dreams
before the crowd is to risk loss.
To love is to risk not being loved in return.
To live is to risk dying.
To hope is to risk despair.
To try is to risk failure.
But risks must be taken because the greatest
tragedy in life is to risk nothing.
The person who risks nothing does
nothing is nothing has nothing.
They may avoid suffering and sorrow but they simply
cannot learn, feel, change, grow, love, live.
Only a person who risks is free.

*– Author Unknown*

**Laura:** I did ok.

*Her friend then spoke up again and said, "She didn't just do ok. She led the team in assists and was second on the team for scoring."*

**Ed:** Are you going to college next year?

**Laura:** Yes.

**Ed:** Are you playing soccer there?

**Laura:** Yes.

*Again, her friend spoke up and interjected, "She got a scholarship to play."*

**Ed:** After looking at all of this can you honestly tell me that you are not a better student and stronger player because you had made that attempt to be captain?

**Laura:** In looking at it now, I am a better person because I made that attempt. I just never thought of looking at it that way.

We get so caught up and focused on the goal that we forget about what we are experiencing and who are becoming on the way toward that goal. Success is a journey not a destination.

## Combination 3:

# Goals

### *Opening the Door to Student Leadership*

On the path of leadership write down your goals and look at them often. Continue to look where you can set mini goals and evaluate your progress along the way. By setting and achieving goals you will have an opportunity to learn a great deal about yourself. Be proud of the goals that you achieve. Remember, it's not just about the goal; it's about who you become and what you experience on your journey towards that goal.

# Action Steps

## Combination 3:
## Goals

OPENING THE DOOR TO
STUDENT LEADERSHIP

## Combination 3:
# Goals

The following action steps are designed for you to practice the combination Goals and open the door to student leadership.

**GOAL:** (gol) *n.* an end that one strives to attain.

> **"Goals and dreams are almost always taller than you are, that way you have to reach to make them come true."**
>
> *– Author Unknown*

Set one goal for yourself following the goal setting formula from this chapter:

- What goal do I want to achieve?

 

 

 

 

- How can I make my goal as specific as possible?

- What resources and skills do I currently have that will help me in reaching my goal?

- What mini goals do I need to set in order to achieve my goal?

- By what date do I want to accomplish each mini goal?

*Combinations*

- By what date do I want to have my major goal achieved?

- Take action with an outstanding attitude and evaluate your progress.

- What is a goal that you have already achieved and how did it make you feel to accomplish it?

- What are some of your dreams?

  _____

  _____

  _____

  _____


- List five qualities that you have that will help
  you in achieving your goals.

  _____

  _____

  _____

  _____


- Create your own quote or inspirational
  thought about Combination 3: GOALS.

  _____

  _____

  _____

  _____

# Leadership Challenge:

Take action toward your goal
in the next 24 hours.

# Respect

"Greatness is not in where we stand, but in what direction we are moving. We must sail sometimes with the wind and sometimes against it – But sail we must, and not drift, nor lie at anchor."

*– Oliver Wendell Holmes*

# A small point makes a big mark

One of my favorite movies of all time is *The Karate Kid*. In that movie Mr. Miyagi taught Daniel the importance of having self respect and respect for others. As a little kid growing up, I didn't have a lot of respect for the people around me. The other kids in my class knew that I had a temper and that I did not know how to control it.

In the third grade when I would get on the bus, many of the kids would sing a song about me. They would yell, "Eddie spaghetti with the meatball eyes, put him in the oven and you get french fries!" In the third grade that was pretty mean stuff! My reaction was to start climbing over the seats of the bus and going after people. As a result, I got kicked off the bus. I did not understand that every choice I made had consequences for which I was responsible.

In the fourth grade, I was in class with all of my friends. One day one of them whispered, "Hey Ed, when Jennifer gets up to go pass in her paper put a couple of tacks on her chair." I replied, "No, I can't do that." "Oh come on Ed, it's just a couple of tacks. We dare you!" I thought my friends would think that I wasn't cool if I did not do it, so I agreed.

Jennifer came back and sat down. Instantly she screamed, but not loud enough for the teacher to hear. My friends started laughing and giving me high-fives. Suddenly, everyone stopped laughing because Jennifer's eyes started to get filled up with tears. She quickly started to wipe the tears away hoping that nobody in the class knew or saw what had just happened – but everybody did. Soon all of my friends went back to do their work, pretending that nothing happened. But I couldn't go back and do my work because I realized what I had just done. My face became very hot and I began to have this sick feeling in my stomach. The type of feeling that you get when you know you are in trouble or you know you have done or said something wrong.

Sensing that something was not right, my teacher called Jennifer up to her desk. After a brief conversation with Jennifer, my teacher stood up and asked our class, "Who would do such a terrible and mean thing to another person?" All of my friends pointed at me and said, "Eddie did it!" The teacher called me out to the hall and in a stern voice said, "Mr. Gerety, young man you will never forget the feeling of guilt and embarrassment that you have right now knowing that what you just did was the wrong thing to do but you did it anyway. Most of all Mr. Gerety," she said tapping me on the shoulder, "that young girl will never forget the pain, embarrassment, and humiliation that you just put her through today."

If I saw Jennifer today, she would still remember that horrible experience in the fourth grade. Every single one of us can remember a time when someone's words or actions really hurt us. It's something that we never forget. The song we learned as little kids, "sticks and stones may break my bones but names will never hurt me" is a big lie. Yes, sticks and stones can break our bones but names and actions can sometimes break our hearts.

On that day in the fourth grade, I suddenly realized that the lack of respect I had for myself and for others was getting me into trouble. It became very clear, that if I was going to be a leader and reach my goals and dreams I had to have respect. I knew in my heart what the right thing was to do and from now on I was going to follow it. I was going to have respect for myself and for others by taking responsibility for the consequences of every choice and decision I made.

**"We are responsible for the consequences of every choice and decision that we make."**

*– Ed Gerety*

The people who told on me were not my friends. Not because they told on me, but because they wanted me to do something that we all knew was the wrong thing to do. In fact, some of our best friends will be those that tell on us when they know that we might hurt ourselves or somebody else. Too many friends do not tell anyone about a destructive choice a friend is making and they end up feeling bad when something happens to their friend. These friends will say things like, "I wish that I told someone about my friend's eating disorder because maybe she wouldn't be so sick," or "I wish that I told someone about my friend's drug addiction because maybe he would not have overdosed," or "I wish I had told someone about my friend's abusive relationship because maybe she wouldn't be in the hospital." A true friend will not pressure you to do something that you believe is wrong and will respect your decision. A true friend will tell a trusted adult if he or she knows that you are hurting yourself or someone else.

**"What you do speaks so loudly
I cannot hear what you say."**

*– Ralph Waldo Emerson*

*Combinations*

## The power to choose

As a student leader, it is important to be aware that there are many different areas that influence the choices and decisions that you make: your friends, family, religion, attitude, the media, past experiences and so on. In every area of our lives we have the power to choose. Every choice will bring us closer to our goals and dreams or further away. Choices ranging from what we allow to be put into our bodies, to how we resolve a conflict, to our goals and dreams, even the relationships in which we get involved.

There are six powerful questions that you can ask yourself when you are about to make a difficult choice or decision:

- Is this choice consistent with what I believe in?

- Am I being influenced in a positive or negative way?

- Will this choice hurt myself or another?

- Will this choice bring me closer to my goals and dreams?

- Will this choice cause me to lose self-respect?

- How will I feel about this choice in one week, in one month, in one year?

Another approach that you can use to make a difficult choice or decision is to consider the following challenges:

**C**learly and specifically
    IDENTIFY the problem.

**H**onestly GATHER as much
    information and resources
    about the problem.

**O**bserve and LIST all possible
    choices and solutions.

**I**mportant: CHOOSE a solution.

**C**onfidently take ACTION.

**E**VALUATE the results.

# Respect for yourself and one another

Several years ago I started taking karate. I walked in the first day and the master of the dojo explained to me that my first lesson would be with the instructor, Dusty. The next thing you know a thirteen year old, with a first-degree black belt, comes walking out of the locker room.

"Are you Ed?" He asked. I looked down at him with a smirk and asked, "Are you Dusty?" He bowed respectfully and said, "Yes, I will be your instructor today." I mockingly patted Dusty on the head and said "Hi Dusty!" and showed him no respect. "Before we start Ed, I just want to quickly show you a special technique." At this point, people had gathered around us waiting to see what would happen. The next thing you know, Dusty had flipped me over his shoulder onto my back on the mat. I couldn't believe what had happened, but I realized that I had made a huge mistake in my judgment about my new instructor. Just because he was small and young didn't mean that I knew everything about him.

One of the responsibilities that you have as a student leader is to be respectful, sensitive, and compassionate not only to the people that you know, but also to the people and the things that you do not know everything about. Is this easy? No, but the only way that we can reach our full potential and be an extraordinary leader is to have respect for yourself and one another.

# *Character*

I would have all young persons taught to respect themselves, their citizenship, the rights of others and all sacred things:

To be healthy, industrious, persevering, provident, courteous, just and honest. Neat in person and in habit, clean in thought and in speech, modest in manner, cheerful in spirit and masters of themselves.

Faithful to every trust, loyal to every duty, magnanimous in judgment, generous in service and sympathetic towards the needy and unfortunate.

For these are the most important things in life and this is not only the way of wisdom, happiness and true success, but the way to make the most of themselves and to be of the greatest service to the world.

*– Albert N. Parlin*

## Actions speak louder than words

In my senior year in high school, I was one of the captains on the varsity football team. During the season, I noticed that one of the players on our team was being picked on by some of our teammates. He was an easy target. His helmet didn't fit right and his extra small shoulder pads were still too big. Whenever the players had a chance they would tackle him extra hard, laughing all the way to the huddle. As one of the leaders on the team, this bothered me. One day, I called some of the players over to the sidelines after practice, and said, "Hey, it's obvious that you guys are a lot stronger and bigger than Adam. We all know he is not as fast and strong as everyone else, so why not take it a little easy on him? He tries hard, respects every player, and is always on time."

"Oh will you relax Ed," they responded, "Come on, he has to pay his dues like everyone else. Don't you remember when we were freshmen? Is this what happens when you become a captain, Gerety?" I didn't know what else to say and I backed down.

Three weeks later, the coach called a team meeting and announced that we had lost a teammate. We all looked around, not sure who was missing. "Adam turned in his pads today," coach said, "he said it was no longer fun." A shot of guilt went through my body because I knew exactly why it wasn't fun for him.

The season went on. We made it to the state championship game that year. During the fourth quarter with 30 seconds left on the clock, our team was up by two touchdowns. The other team called a time out and we began to celebrate our team's first state championship in school history. I went to the sidelines to look for my family and friends, but the first person I noticed in the bleachers was Adam. We looked at each other for a second, and not knowing what else to do, I gave him a nod with my head. I felt guilty for a moment, but I was quickly caught up again in the celebration.

Two weeks later my Mom saw Adam's mother in the grocery store. She began to tell my mom how much she wished that Adam had stayed on the team. "He was so proud and excited to be a football player," she said. "He would get up early in the morning just to make sure that he had all of his gear together for practice. He loved being able to say to his younger brother and sister that he was part of the team."

When my mom came home and told me what Adam's mom had said, I felt terrible. Although I was not one of the players who had bullied Adam, I had done nothing to stop it. I didn't stand up tall enough or strong enough to put an end to how Adam was being treated. I realized that day that as a leader, it is my responsibility to make everybody feel a part of the team or organization that I am involved in and to make sure that each person is treated with respect.

# Combination 4:

# Respect

## *Opening the Door to Student Leadership*

An important part of the combination of respect is to lead by example. It is not what we say, but what we do. As a leader, your words and your actions can do two things – they can build people up or tear people down. Respect yourself. Great leaders have a respect for themselves and for one another. Know that you have the power to choose in every moment of your life and you are responsible for the consequences of your choices.

# Action Steps

## Combination 4:
## Respect

OPENING THE DOOR TO
STUDENT LEADERSHIP

*Ed Gerety*

## Combination 4:
# Respect

The following action steps are designed for you to practice the combination RESPECT and open the door to student leadership.

**RESPECT:** (ri spekt') *v.* to show consideration for.

---

> **"How we respect ourselves and one another is a true representation of our character and ultimately whether or not we turn our dreams into a reality."**
>
> *– Mark Gerety*

---

- Share a time when you made a judgment about a person or situation without knowing all the information. How did it make you feel?

- Why is it important to take a step back before you react to a situation or person?

- Share a time when you made a choice to not do something that your friends wanted you to do? What did you learn about yourself from this experience?

*Combinations*

- List three friends who respect your choices and support you for being yourself. What qualities do they have?

_____

_____

_____

_____

- What is something you could do that would show respect for yourself?

_____

_____

_____

_____

- What are three things that you could do to show respect for others?

_____

_____

_____

_____

- Create your own quote or inspirational thought about Combination 4: RESPECT.

*Combinations*

# Leadership Challenge:

Watch the movie,
*The Karate Kid*
(1984 rated PG)
or the movie,
*Dead Poet's Society*
(1989 rated PG).

# 5

# Kindness

**"Kind words can be short and easy to speak, but their echoes are truly endless."**

*– Mother Theresa*

*Combinations*

# The Golden Rule

When I was growing up, my parents taught me how important it was to be kind to others. The golden rule: to treat others as you would like to be treated. It's inspiring to know that right now, teenagers all over the world like you are making a positive difference in their schools, in their community, and in the world.

## A pledge for kindness

Maggie, a high school student in Indiana, was tired of hearing the put-downs and seeing the bullying that was going on in her school. She and her friends decided that they were going to do something about it. They were convinced that they could make a difference and they wanted to prove it.

**"What act of kindness can you do today to make a difference?"**

*– Ed Gerety*

With the help of their student council and the support of their principal, they put into action a special program called the Frankton Pledge. In this pledge, the students make a promise to replace put-downs with positive communication. They had a candle lighting ceremony in the gym and students were given the opportunity to share stories of how words and actions hurt them or a friend in the past. Every one was given a ribbon and then the following pledge was made:

*I will pledge a personal commitment to become more tolerant of other's differences. I will avoid put downs of others and instead replace them with a more positive form of communication.*

*I will pledge a personal commitment to become a member of the helping majority that becomes a friend to other students being taunted. If others won't become part of the solution, I will.*

It is this type of effort that can make a positive difference in someone's life and make your school a better place. It is not just large acts of kindness that can make a difference. It's the little things. A simple hello, a smile or a kind word can make another person's day.

## Making a difference

When Miranda was a senior in high school she decided to write a letter to her friends about believing in yourself and following your heart. "I'm not an expert on life. I have not even lived to see twenty years, but I'm not naïve either. Things have happened that have made me a stronger person – these are some things that I know. Never try to be something you are not. You will just be living a lie and will not be happy with yourself. Secondly, listen to your heart, both in circumstances you are faced with, and about your own body. The inner voice that you hear knows a lot more than you think. Thirdly, never take anything for granted. Life is beautiful."

Miranda knows that in order to open the door to a successful life there are combinations that you need to remember and continue to use if you are going to make your dreams come true.

Student leaders have shared with me the following acts of kindness that you can do to make a difference:

Put spare change in a strangers
expired meter.

Bake a cake for the teachers at
your school to say "thank you."

When going through a tollbooth, pay
for the person behind you.

Bake cookies and deliver them to
the nursing home in your town.

Let someone go in front of you
while waiting in line.

Send a friend a funny or thoughtful card.

Donate clothes to a homeless shelter.

Volunteer at your church.

Clean up the house to surprise
your parents.

Plant flowers in a run down area of town.

## What act of kindness can you do today that would make a difference?

**"Some people come into our lives and quickly go, others stay a while and leave footprints in our hearts and we are never, ever the same."**

*– Eleanor Roosevelt*

# Little Champions

Have you ever listened to the news, read the paper, or heard a story that prompted you to do something about it? Maybe you didn't know quite where to start but somehow you knew that even doing something small could make a difference.

This is exactly how the little champions project began.

Suzanne wanted to make a difference in her community. There were children in the area who were not able to participate in athletic programs because they could not afford the expensive equipment. Not wanting any child to be left out from the joy and fun of sports, Suzanne created the little champions project. She asked community leaders and her church to help her collect new and used sports equipment.

The response was amazing! In just one weekend over three hundred pieces of equipment were collected. The generosity of the community and Suzanne's desire to make a difference impacted hundreds of local children. They received baseball gloves, bats, soccer balls, cleats, hockey skates, basketballs and more. Suzanne will never meet all the children for whom her project made a difference. The ripple effect of her actions can never be measured.

Look around your school, your community, and your world to see where you can reach out and make a difference.

## *Watch your thoughts*

Watch your thoughts…

They become your words.

Watch your words…

They become your actions.

Watch your actions…

They become your habits.

Watch your habits…

Your habits become your character.

Watch your character…

It becomes your destiny.

*– Frank Outlaw*

## Combination 5:

# Kindness

### *Opening the Door to*
### *Student Leadership*

Every day you have an opportunity to reach out and make a difference through your words and actions: a simple smile, a friendly hello, or a helping hand. You may never know the impact that your kindness can have on another. Never let those that do not respond in kind stop you from leading with your heart.

# Action Steps

## Combination 5:
## Kindness

### OPENING THE DOOR TO
### STUDENT LEADERSHIP

## Combination 5:
# Kindness

The following action steps are designed for you to practice the combination KINDNESS and open the door to student leadership.

**KINDNESS:** (kind ness) *n.* the state, quality or habit of being kind.

---

> **"It is when we truly give of ourselves**
> **that we realize the true meaning of life**
> **and all of the possibilities that it holds."**
>
> *– Joanne Gerety Rice*

---

- Share an example of a time when someone went out of their way to be kind to you?

- Describe five things that make you smile or happy.

- Name three places in your school or community that you could volunteer your time and make a difference.

- Give an example of how you can be kind to yourself.

- Create your own inspirational quote or saying about Combination 5: KINDNESS.

# Leadership Challenge:

Compliment five people and do three
acts of kindness anonymously.

# Believe

**"If you can dream it, you can do it."**

*– Walt Disney*

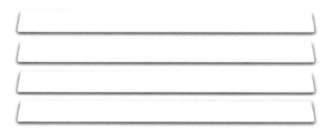

*Combinations*

# A dream come true

One year I went to watch my brother compete in a popular triathlon held in Falmouth, Massachusetts. This triathlon was a half-mile swim in the ocean, a 26.2-mile bike ride, and then a 6.2-mile sprint run to the finish line.

Before my brother and the other racers jumped into the ocean, another competitor went in first. His name is Mr. Richard Hoyt. I watched as Mr. Richard Hoyt picked up his son Rick who has cerebral palsy. Rick cannot run or walk. Mr. Hoyt laid his son down into a specially made raft and then wrapped two strong straps around his waist and over his shoulder and jumped into the Atlantic Ocean. He swam the half-mile distance towing his son behind him in the raft.

*Never give up on your dreams.*

**"In the journey through life
you are never alone.
There are people to help you
along the way."**

*– Ed Gerety*

Mr. Hoyt got out of the ocean, picked up his son, who weighs over 150 pounds, and ran seventy-five yards across the deep sand with his son in his arms. He then put Rick on the front of his racing bike into a special seat. Mr. Hoyt biked the 26.2-mile bike ride competitively with his son in front of him.

*In the journey through life you are never alone.*
*There are people to help you along the way.*

Right after the 26.2-mile bike race, Mr. Hoyt placed his son into a chair with wheels on it and pushed his son the remaining 6.2-mile sprint run to the finish line.

In an interview on television a reporter asked Mr. Hoyt, "Why do you do what you do?" Mr. Hoyt answered, "One day somebody said that my son did not know what it was like to compete. One day somebody said that I could not do what it was that I wanted to do. My son Rick and I, our whole family, we are a team and we work together. We believe in one another. We love one another and because of that we are able to do what it is that we do."

*Believe in one another.*

# Teenagers Are Amazing

Teenagers are amazing,
I wish the world could see,
just how beautiful we are,
how compassionate we can be.

I wish they could take back,
all the cynical things they've said,
and see how much we shine,
be positive instead.

Remark on our radiant smiles,
and the differences we make,
all of the people our lives have touched,
all of the chances that we take.

Notice how we change,
each and every day,
wanting to leave childhood,
yet desperately wanting to stay.

I wish they could remember,
how tough our lives can be,
the promises that are broken,
the violence that we see.

Yet still we venture onward,
unsure of where the road may lead,
hoping they will take notice,
hoping they'll take heed,
of the changes that we've made,
of the power that we hold,
of the wisdom we have hidden,
of the stories yet untold.

I hope the world will notice,
what some have already seen,
teenagers are amazing people,
striving to follow their dreams.

*– Jamie Haskins*

## Personal best

Ali was a junior in high school when she was diagnosed with a rare form of cancer. She had a tumor removed from her stomach, about the size of a softball. Throughout her battle with cancer, she had support from her family, friends, and doctors. Although the chemotherapy sessions were scary for Ali, the belief and courage that lied within enabled her to persevere.

In her senior year, Ali was not selected to be the captain of her basketball team. She had missed too many practices and was far behind in her classes due to cancer treatments. She remained positive knowing that the real victory was not in titles, awards, and recognition but rather giving her personal best.

Ali's cancer is now in remission. She may not have "captain" on her basketball uniform or an asterisk next to her name to designate high honors, but is clear that she has leader written across every word that she writes and every step that she takes. She lives her life with a belief and courage that I know lies inside of you.

> **"You miss 100% of the shots
> you don't take."**
>
> *–Wayne Gretzky*

# Rising to the challenge

"I can't make it," she cried, "My arms are tired and my knee hurts. Please pull me up!!!"

These were the words that echoed off the Otter Cliffs in Acadia National Park from Alexis, a sixteen year old, during her first rock climbing experience. It was towards the end of the day and six other students on the trip had all repelled the 90-foot cliff. The cliff went straight down onto a charcoal black rock ledge, which then descended into the Atlantic Ocean. All of the students had successfully rock climbed back up and Alexis was the last to go. She was a strong-minded, sensitive kid who had lately found herself getting into trouble at school and at home. There had been no specific reason for this recent behavior except that she was feeling stressed out and overwhelmed with everything. She had come on this trip because a friend of hers had said that it would be a good time and that it might help her to figure some things out.

Each time she thought her hand or foot had found a new crevice or a new spot to move her upwards, she would slip and fall only to have the climbing harness catch her. Alexis was hot and tired. The chalk from her hands was beginning to get in her eyes. With rage in her voice she yelled, "Pull me up! I quit. I hate this. This is stupid!"

It was at that moment when Jason, the head counselor on the trip, looked at me and said, "Ed, I'm going to go down and talk with her."

I then yelled down to Alexis, "Hold on! You can do this. We know you can!"

Jason grabbed another rope, put his climbing harness on and began to repel down the cliff. Within moments Jason was beside Alexis. She had her cheek directly against the face of the rock with her feet barely resting on a small piece of the cliff that jetted outward. Jason said to Alexis, "I know that you have been on this cliff now for what seems like a very long time. Your feet and fingers are cramping up and your forearms feel as though they are on fire. But, Alexis, you are strong, look how far up you are already. You have taken one of the more difficult paths up the cliff. Look Alexis, look at the path you have taken."

At that moment, Alexis moved her cheek away from the rock face and looked down. The bright white chalk she used on her hands to give her a better grip, showed the trail where her tired hands had moved upward on the cliff. Jason was right; Alexis had taken the hardest way up the cliff. Jason then looked straight into Alexis' eyes and in a calm voice he said, "You are not alone out here, there are people who care about you, who want to help you and see you succeed. We are going to do this together. Are you ready?" Hesitantly, she shook her head yes and took a deep breath.

The secret to getting up the cliff is to take it one step at a time. Sometimes we are in such a rush to get to the top that we miss a spot that will help us move a step closer to our goal. It's ok to fall and slip, even to rest, as log as you begin climbing again no matter how many times you fall.

"Alexis, I know that you can do this, you know that you can do this." Words of encouragement began to echo down from the students up above as Alexis began to slowly crawl upwards. Jason was right beside her as she made each move. He was not telling her where to go or what to do. Instead, he was reminding her of the power that she had within her to get to the top. You see, sometimes we forget that we already have the power and the resources to help us reach our goals. At any moment in our lives we can tap into that power and reach a new level. Only if we are willing to take the risk to let go of what is familiar and secure in our lives, and reach out to something that is new and different.

"Almost there, hold on, hang in there, you can do it, don't give up!" Finally, with one last pull by her tired hands, Alexis found herself on top of the cliff. She was greeted by high fives, slaps on the back, and wide-eyed smiles.

**"Today represents another opportunity
on the road to greatness."**

*– Ralph Waldo Emerson*

Looking back on her first experience at rock climbing, Alexis said that the event reminded her of where she was right now in her life, somewhat unsure of where to go next. She needed to remind herself to continue to move forward and that she was not alone in dealing with the pressures that she was going through. Alexis is like most kids her age. She is trying to do well in school and find a group of friends that will bring out the best in her. A group of friends that will accept her for the person that she is. She hopes to make the varsity softball team and be accepted into a good college. Out there on the cliff, Alexis was reminded that there were people there to help her. Rock climbing is very much like life. Each person chooses her own path and that is what makes it so special and rewarding. The lessons that we learn in life are taught to us in so many different ways. They could be through the adventure of rock climbing, an unexpected experience with a close friend, being part of a team, or even right in a classroom.

## Seeds of wisdom

When I visited a first grade classroom, the first thing I noticed when I walked into the room were the tiny seats. They sat low under neatly arranged desks. The entire classroom was covered in colorful art. Each picture had the student's name written on it in bold letters, which showed how proud they were of their work. The teacher said, "Class, please put down your pencils and say hello to our special guest, Mr. Gerety."

All of a sudden, eighteen of the cutest little kids you have ever seen said in unison, "Helloooooo Mr. Gerety."

I asked, "How are you today, class?" They all responded, "Gooooood!!"

The teacher then said to me, "Mr. Gerety, come over here and sit down."

I then heard a couple of the kids whisper, "Cool, he gets to sit in the special chair."

I was guided to the corner of the classroom, which was the reading center, and I sat down into an old wooden rocking chair. The eighteen first graders all sat around me and I asked, "Does anyone have any questions?"

Boom!! Almost all the hands shot up into the air with sounds of, "oh, oh, I do, I do!" Quickly, I called on one student. I asked her name and after a long pause she said, "Kelly," somewhat unsure of her answer.

I asked, "What is your question Kelly?"

"Is it true, how come, ummm, oops I forgot."

"That's okay, I'll come back to you later." I asked another, "What is your name?"

He answered, "Chip."

"What is your question Chip?" He asked, "Mr. Gerety, do you want to see what it is we are doing?"

I said, "Sure Chip." The next thing I know, Chip stood up and walked to the windowsill of the classroom. I got up and followed Chip. Seventeen other kids got up and followed me. Chip reached to the windowsill and pulled down a milk carton, which was cut in half. He held it the way you and I would hold a newborn baby. Carefully, he moved closer to me and said with excitement in his voice, "Look Mr. Gerety, look what we're doing."

The milk carton was filled half way with dirt, and a little green thing was coming out of the center. Now, excitedly I said, "Wow! What are you doing in there, growing a pine tree?"

Chip just shook his head and replied, "No Mr. Gerety, we are growing a flower."

"Tell me Chip, how did you grow that flower?" He said, "First thing we had to do, Mr. Gerety, is get some good dirt, not bad dirt, but good dirt."

I said, "Ok Chip, then what happened?"

"Well, everyone in the class was given one seed and the teacher said we better not eat it, because we were not getting another. We then had to plant the seed one-fingernail length beneath the soil. But see Mr. Gerety," as he put his finger half an inch from my nose, "I had to go a whole knuckle length because my finger is so small."

I said, "I can see Chip. Then what happened?"

"Then we had to give it a little bit of water, a little bit of sun, but not too much."

"When do you check on it?"

"Before snack and after recess."

I held up the milk carton to look for Chip's name on the bottom of it, but his name was not on it. In fact, there was no name on it at all, so I looked at him and asked, "Chip, is this flower yours?"

He said, "Yes," then he said, "well no."

I asked, "Well, which one is it?"

He said, "I'm not sure."

"You're not sure?" I said, loudly. "You mean to tell me, Chip, that the seventeen other milk cartons all along that windowsill, not one of them has a name on it?"

He said, "No, Mr. Gerety."

I asked, "Then tell me Chip, how do you know which one is whose?" Chip looked up at me, kind of surprised that I did not know the answer and said, "Well, we don't Mr. Gerety. We just take care of every one." Then the little boy next to him responded enthusiastically, "Then we get to take them home."

The important lessons that were being taught to those first graders are as important today as they were in the first grade. They are the importance of working together, supporting one another, and believing in something even at first if you cannot see it.

# Combination 6:

# Believe

### *Opening the Door to*
### *Student Leadership*

Through school and throughout your entire life there will be wonderful, joyful moments when you feel as though everything is perfect. There will also be times in your life when you are going to be faced with set backs, disappointments, and things that don't turn out the way you expect them to. It is during these times when you need to remember that you have the power to believe in yourself and to make the choice not to give up, and that you are not alone. There are people who care about you, who want to help you, and who love you very much. So continue to explore, dream, and discover all that lies ahead of you in this great journey of life.

## Combination 6:
## Believe

## OPENING THE DOOR TO
## STUDENT LEADERSHIP

## Combination 6:
# Believe

The following action steps are designed for you to practice the combination BELIEVE and open the door to student leadership.

**BELIEVE:** (be lev') *v.* to have confidence or trust.

> **"I am convinced that my life belongs to the whole community: and as long as I live, it is my privilege to do for it whatever I can, for the harder I work, the more I live. I rejoice in life for its own sake. Life is no brief candle to me. It is a sort of splendid torch, which I got hold of for a moment, and I want to make it burn as brightly as possible before turning it over to future generations."**
>
> *– George Bernard Shaw*

- Describe a time in your life when you showed courage. What have you learned about yourself from that experience?

- How do you want to be remembered?

- What are five things you believe?

- What do you believe are your strengths/ talents?

_____

_____

_____

_____

- Create your own inspirational quote or saying about Combination 6: BELIEVE.

_____

_____

_____

_____

# Leadership Challenge:

Read the book,
*It's Not About the Bike*,
by Lance Armstrong.

COMBINATION

# Summary

# COMBINATIONS
## OPENING THE DOOR TO STUDENT LEADERSHIP

As you continue to grow as a leader, remember to lead with **GRATITUDE;** an appreciation for your abilities and the people in your life,

With that gratitude, you will begin to develop the right kind of **ATTITUDE,**

which will empower you to take action to set and achieve your **GOALS**.

Your power in being a leader lies within your ability to have **RESPECT** for yourself and one other. You are responsible for the consequences of your choices and decisions. Lead by example and lead with your heart.

Continue to reach out and make a difference knowing that the impact of your **KINDNESS** can never be measured.

It takes great courage to be a leader and no matter where you go, always **BELIEVE**.

*Ed Gerety*

# Recommended Reading List

*It's Not About the Bike,* Lance Armstrong: © 2000 Penguin USA

*Teen Power* **series**, Eric Chester, et. al. ChesPress Publications

*The 7 Habits of Highly Effective Teens*, Sean Covey: © 1998 Fireside

*Life By Design*, Nancy Hunter Denney: © 2000 Victory Inc.

*Playing Beyond The Scoreboard*, Craig Hillier: © 2002 Winning Edge Publications

*When Bad Things Happen To Good People*, Rabbi Harold Kushner: © 1989 Shocken

*Fired Up*, Snowden McFall: © 1997 Success Publishers

*Life Strategies For Teens*, Jay McGraw: © 2000 Simon and Schuster

*Way Of The Peaceful Warrior*, Dan Millman: © 1984 Berkley

*Never Die Easy*, Walter Payton: © 2000 Random House

*Power of Positive Thinking*, Norman Vincent Peale: © 1992 Fawcett

*Triumph Over Tragedy*, Bobby Petrocelli: © 1995 WRS Publishing

*Awaken the Giant Within*, Anthony Robbins: © 1992 Fireside

*The Four Agreements*, Don Miguel Ruiz: © 1997 Amber Allen Publishing

*The Psychology of Winning*, Denis Waitley: © 1984 Berkley

For further suggestions check out

**www.GeretyPresentations.com**

**WHALEBACK**
PUBLISHING

*a subsidiary of
Gerety Presentations*

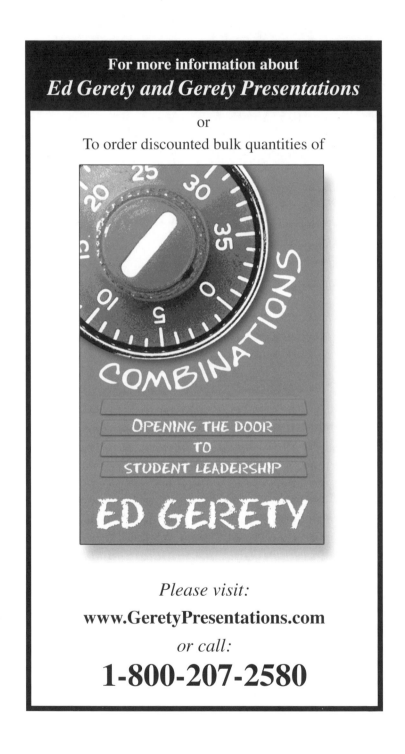